Chainsaw (

MW01230948

Poems

by

Keith Higginbotham

COMMUNICATIONS

©2023
Keith Higginbotham
LJMcD Communications

ISBN: 9798372049055

All rights reserved. No part of this book may be reproduced without express written permission of the author.

Cover: detail from *Arab Figures in Oasis* by Lachlan J McDougall

Ipswich, Queensland, Australia

Contact LJMcD Communications:
lachlan.mcdougall@gmail.com

COMMUNICATIONS

CONTENTS

Pole Job

Sal Mineo

Whose Benjamin

Idaho

World Shit Mask

Space Factory

Mod for the Cardigan

Shirt of Nails

Wooden Bug

Strobe Pagoda

Three Walls

Bubble

Mammals

Marginalia

Furry Rocket

Rooms of Giant Piss

Blows the Trope

Nerve Photo

Smocked

Warhead

Flood Machine

Nagasaki

Pluto's Pardoned His Flowers

Some of these poems originally appeared in experiential-experimental-literature, Otoliths, and The Zoomoozophone Review

Introduction

I first came across Keith when he submitted some poems to a little magazine I was editing by the name of *D.O.R.* His mastery of form and syntax were unparalleled—where most poets were careening off into wild arenas, Keith was here tactfully curtailing his rushing gusts of feeling and reigning in the madness to small, containable poems that explode like landmines.

What we have here is a fantastic collection of heavily programmed poems that contain entire universes in their constrained lines. Where some prefer to blast out into the bombastic reaches, Keith burrows down into the heart and soul of the mundane becoming madness. Each poem is a little gem that reflects the light in a sparkling rainbow if you just hold it up in a certain way—his language is a prism and it is up to you to figure it out. That is not to say that these poems are difficult. They may have their element of archaeology, but really they are simple affairs containing the world of abstraction. The language washes over you in warm waves and gives you the room to come back for more and more finding something new each time you have a look.

I am extremely happy to have been sent this collection. It warms my heart to see poets who are this dedicated to the form while still being willing to push the boundaries and explore the outer reaches. Keith is firmly a modernist. His poems are microcosms of the modern world wrapped up in a genuine love for the form of poetry.

Read on and see what I mean—maybe some of his love will rub off on you!

Lachlan J McDougall

Limitations

What we're holding on
to is holding us
back: carbon house, home
on the radio, orchestral
through this
terminology of appliance
wealth.

Add mutual replicate and show
the play, sideways, as if
negative to denote
a common
depiction of working
is problematic.

And so the future
warms, countenance
a mere practice of motif
in reducing; annoy the twain.

Recite the randomized
approach, Son of Label: This is
the era of birth order, flax,
and taboo.

More Someone

I was all nothingness and everything,
a glass there in the counterfeit wash.
I was a man of brownstones. I lived
in the flesh of lobbies, walked the
psychic avenues, waiting for the great
future-past, like mold. Remembering
smudge. Skin rash. Boiled style blob
soul beet for shoes. I got more metallic.
October's holes blew a circus in. I
turned a turntable. Tongue clubbed.
Abysmal orange heresies in symbols.
We jacked the fluid night all up in
black apropos of the mistake
machine—we brought a dirty flag.
We cranked the miming sound lacing
the orchard turned in blank mood
cures. All my arms wheeled away.

Five Giant Eyes

infinite time sky;
umbrellas from tombstones
all masculine like
a manufactured
selfish drift & the and

there is sound
in ends

he kites his polymer
mirrors bright like sex
& sweep; & arm-
twisting

I recorded a room
of oaks
shoplifting
into mountains

Hello, I Must Be Going

Thinking astride the paradise that
platforms in the 18th century: the depths
of dismal afternoons unwashed
in unwavering parlance. My reaction
is a bastard of leaves reading
the moderns. The drowsy language
crucifies itself in my head,
the emperor's subway dissolves,
noise of the glass chambered
skin slips in. The motion of byways.
The motion of pagan labor.
Drawers of history wear over all
gesturing. Threadlike western genres
slice the message.

Prosthetic Nature

Like rows in cylinders and together all radiation
Is recalled lines. Aurora the
Very ear of the wake.
Radio off. Screaming in a room of historic
Equations.
Mouth the word *blue*. Off,
Off in the keystone. Off a nail,
Photocopies of deer
And bison. Wake up terrifying
Grassland.
We skip
The family ritual singing
Off the drum line.

Amsterdam Avenue

Coast of escapes
cold-water balls the
moon realm
that foams a hole down
expels the battery
in a boxcar
and lives beyond
seabirds camembert
in hydrogen jazz
anecdotal war the cities
of the Indians
are all beards
and bears
and rooms rolling toward
roaring sex in
the backyard drive
breaks the doom
of cowardly miles
in holy subways
and gymnasiums
holy peyote in dusk
wheels the
angry rock dreams
brilliant in
glacier hotels
meat water the joyride
crime in the academies
the clogged noise
detectives of a million
submarine slopes
of the busted American
universe.

Porkpie

His embrued hands;
Great big saint which things
           Salvation in;
           (with sinn'd and
           crown'd
           and bestrewed)
Land salvation.
A hand grave found?
           (doth mind
           a grave.)

Still lukewarm his brethren
Referenced dissembling thou his strife
           (and not by word cast;
Gates of Holiness words
I crave);
Referenced his praying excess
           Of terrors.

Thus all civil country saints
           (whose crimes wind
           England's twin)
Beware the great blemish flaming
Upon the wheel undone.

Three Poems

1.

misplaced oboe, the
sun back so naughty

bites the village on
your numbered ledge

2.

afternoon iron vein shirts all,
hours sister the town

3.

home itself in the grim

unsteepled rust squeals
hands of swivel
blood wheels the glass trees

Four Poems

1.

Swan of days
there's a bacterial
                    feeling

territorial

            hence wings

2.

Eroded ash
hammered down

done with

3.

Feathers kneeling
                    heaven in

a poor explanation
                        white

punctured sunlight

4.

An inverted kitchen
against rhyme

                    silent
geometry

Popsicle

in the headlight
revivals gas lots foot-longs

the never growth the weightless
old whole wilderness bores

across settlement's green sweater
characters ground the arrows around

a machine called land bats the last
glass hold of promise

your unlucky western trail threads gone
from piano all of rotgut blessing

remember father's man land
characters gone to saddlebags his

distance creeps to swallowed dust
toward the spidering shore

the lonelier I play the longing hold
beautiful pulse in the forked hand

History Teaches

Newsprint of empty shoulders
in the grassed arm

Skin stacked on the scattered
autumn hair full of head

Chubby Flag

hang my teeth   slit faced
rolled in valleys   to wind
as hands   piss me
up   up the pole

Giant

The man no. 754 is dented
            from metal
            can in fire skyline the

The the the   chrysanthemum power

Giant black chicken-of-the-woods

Orange Birds

skies frozen
hanging down

the crushed
stairway

boats flooded
on language

in needles of
elderly jungles

high on diamond
buildings

dithering in
the conversation

of auto-tongue
hair in

the red maze
satellite tea

wooden oceans
of knives inside

her neck
knot a favorite

town of mirrors
background of

bath the marble
beyond our

televised flowers

my pastel hat

wings eating light

Meringue

The fish from pedal climate
downwards altogether in sky deprivation;
a hollyhock
tins the eyeball.

The head is less phallic and
faces north storming
vowelless windows and
the street distorts hyper
dollops end
underground past the embedded
mountainsides.

A head – circle the inverted occasional
world with anonymous
centers, locate the intolerable
and perfect the bravos.

The occasional reflection
ensconced up onto who
is most oblivious,
the night in
meringue – inside what
parasols.

Ant Stars

Seemingly—;
Others that mistake — clouds;
.
For the barely rosy—; a
Doppelgänger;

So with; with—ant stars;
Floor used of flat hooves;

Symbols all swimming in;
The color of volcanic

Blank.

The Hanged Father

the delicate pale
arrives in fall the end of the end of

resurfaced window of death like a wind
woods it

the hanged father is a he
mute so buries so

wearing cement near tresses
like silence was old was that

old man

Breathe Earth

Time envelope shackles in
apathy of the lingering ring.
Yodeling there on the
away.

Slurred resurrection intones
the complaint of hardened
scenery. All repeating
is amended, for you are
the boastful fountain we room
rainbows around. You're
the anarchy bridge.

In shadows, velvet tourists drip
unhinged words, outputting the hymn
of complicity. Upfalling layers
park your shave. Claw-clouds blank into
cupcakes' flesh, the fingers
own the edge.

Aeroplane

big eyes encased in
　　　moontop on lap as on
　　　　　the eminem

　　　　　converged
　　　consciousness of
filament villas big

　　　of something

mornings spent in preparation of
　　　post sunset suicides
　　　　　misguided

　　　　　lightning
　　　the afternoons
about light

Beat

St. Cather's lawn skull returning king money turpentine;
sun racketing wastebaskets the lives battered
within the hall aromatic, central steaming listening on lost
wake
benzedrine and you are the empty night; it's winter in
Jersey.
The migraine awakes high burdens and knees its birdcalls.

Dawn is the impulse to cross poverty in the Bronx.
Farms trees and roof thickets where union skeletons gloss
into
dark dreams drank platonic intoxication windows,
ferry of hell nightmares the heaven smell among hours;
idling chipping green universities who float again the

alcohol the incomparable lightning followed light all the
way
to Paterson, big clean burning Paterson illuminating starry
lights of dungarees and drugs and hush the sea-lion land
that ran around the ashcan of wilderness naked, cooked
skin dragging a piano breathing lonesome hysterical
freeway.

Shock Study

pelt buildings, cigars wash, locked subjects, sickened
roadside
senseless vagrant
fluorescent bone
bulls eyes

ripe drowning, nothing mocked, flame strips
drink collapse
drink wind
drink spoken sand

wax holidays, door staunch, static looped, brown laugh
benign hat, liquid skin
talking coat
the same questions

surprise inelegantly, feathered flesh, heft habitat, fallen
jokes
nails bloom
soil happiness
vote lung again

On Animal Globe Abyss His

on animal globe abyss his
illiterate manacles have unpasted
the two the always the sequins to
anyone on with weather with
the wherewithal of
these unlettered lungs the dead
feather the snow flesh the
fur blooms the order of the I

Pole Job

slick bridges st
and
on the thorn
the thorn smoke
s the sky the
phone the
quarantined holes
the wrecking
gesture the mac
kerel towns the electric
fields and
seas and farms and
interstates the car
s check
er the pole the
mind life smack
ed in cheese lug
gage the long
mountain throttles
the nightly train

Sal Mineo

sal mineo was made of clay
as illusive as a poem sal mineo
was from the dark future
he grew on the paper the poem
was written on and sal
mineo was the capital
of inevitability the captain of
unknown spaces sal mineo was
both a son and a daughter
sal mineo played one on TV
and when it was time sal
mineo bombed his own
house in the hills sal mineo rode
a horse into the town
sal mineo was kind to the poor
and sal mineo never asked for
what was coming and eventually sal
mineo took off all his clothes

Whose Benjamin

myth music manner wrist
angels clamshell past
his cleopatra day goal

has pens proceed and nearly
parting the days
with water

in the arcades
garage flowers
decompose erasures

on amended screens
cat logic the asphalt
coleridge's people said

Idaho

dear sea inside clowns that discovered your shadows
drew persuaded roads of secretaries so neat in their
enterprises
the cheering young rogue saw the light in heaven closed

having cannot have anymore from not walking on wings
dictating god the split of all yachting the canned van of
peaks
riven mouth thread through with letters you dream
of archetype streets through the town shaken all out
to out with infantries in

round two of symphonies shatter on in dictation the bridge
of forest
which fences in all the darlings the night a broken colon of
the remained
re-enacted faces of comic book appeasement all the
hallways of
humans gone

not a blessing forsaken together already trees the distance
to beds
this our finished past ghosting the doling forest I free
ghosting the empress holidays ghosting blank snakes in

World Shit Mask

Through fraudulent shadows
Expect sinew/;
       buildings homesick
       the high salient struggling,
       a bag
Of butchers in a chair,

Kingdom of lowbrow anthems
Airbrush the séances, unbearable grasses
Of peppered scars.

Mirror on the mouth making things worse.
It's no mirror,
       said the Southern
       gunshot
       spun toward applause.

Space Factory

bag of twisted eyes
        a grass ballet
on a chair back black
meteors of the future
down on a deacon's plate
        homemade road-
sides murder the narratives
through the wall
of television
        sleeves of teenage
soldiers junk the hotel
all in a dinner theater
set underwater

Mod for the Cardigan

In the absence of typos
the aristocracy of cross-country bodies
embroidered the avenue. This
is a given. I was all
coffee-stained, my brain
brushed under the floorboards
in the season of feasting.

I had rogue memories of foraging
for segues, lullabies in
the hinterlands, mass lapses
of vulgar language
under the skin of naked
classmates.

Yawning over the missing
catalogues all
misty-eyed, I burned my teenage
brand in your table
of inventions. Our forefathers
therefore, their empire of
crucified gadgets
and bongs, bent unhinged
in their fragilities.

Shirt of Nails

people in the hills of flame
in flamboyant garden walls
clueless as themselves

in armoires in the distant memories
in the holes of archipelagos
in the carpets of gesturing nurses

hallmark a diagnostic ball
even in mid-action—running
with the history of afternoons

in the name you bleed

Wooden Bug

Wooden bug. Winged skin
on tail read sky facet
glass jazz; live whiskey
covering Missoula
rattles gasoline white with
constant windowsill, pouring
rafters through rioting.
Two space lavender museums
hillside sorting these
lost bleats. Never mind
the classroom.

Brown portraits in our room.
Our room—the category of
myself. Elevators ant
cans into crushes
of tunnels. The beach
is drooling. The beach is
drooling more. And landscape
in vanished flutter.
Tape the teeth to
the red sea doors. Turquoise
heads limp inside
sleeping but the
rain boat has been changing
words.

Plays of paper on
the gutted table. Belly from
the famous mezzanine to blotches.
Sleeping of asphalt blue
curling ladder of
the needle out in the
darkness launching
skyscrapers. Green
televisions through its doll
from bags of blooms.

A tile pile to be
broken into an old friend.
See the cliffs flush.

In the sky
wrestle. Dreams now
unfurl in the scummy
valley. Abandoned
neighborhoods of neon
children swinging barn
planks. Recordings disappear.
The neon school weaponized
like a flag, jumps out
of the stories. Finds the space
lounge the books
scream against. On the table
a wooden bug.

Strobe Pagoda

Stone water.

Flesh satellite drifting in.
The odor of
               syllables red.

Gas dream
               circulates the faces of sky;

sky falling glass satellite morning grey from stone
the terminal smell of typewriter flares

whistling in bodies.

Three Walls

Quit the paper, a parable of
gender swipes. Hair a backdrop of

tiny orange expanse. We cranked
a wordsmith from behind.

An elaborate robotic moment can
articulate a silly innocence

anytime, collected in the back.
Reverie an homage to a giant

whizzing sound, palette of the deadpan
antique shroud minus the chain-link sun.

Bubble

big eyes encased in
       moontop on lap as on
           the eminem

        converged
      consciousness of
filament villas big

     of something

mornings spent in preparation of
      post sunset suicides
        misguided

        lightning
   the afternoons
about light

Mammals

with log skies the
armpit tucked
in a hero's wake, with
labyrinths the
telephone torn homeward
the grounded book
returns, celestial of down
go down lie him in
a daylight of directions
we fought denouement beyond
earth's depths way fall
in the liquid place
obscuring the mindset
of brown breath rocks
heal the archaic sympathy

Marginalia

this hell—a balmy buckskin-brown house
out in the objections

read: raft-building, underlined in pencil
wedding the drums like a born-again road

over the great forties an abbreviated memoir
from this affect we have to extract context

while artificial hand-speed changes the political,
changes movement from chaos to precursor—

direct primitive invariants found in the tapping
yard, the mind's infinite characters

on artistic grounds, a mouth of antidote
surrounds the stamina of critical nodes

buckshot, be chosen, and hand off the criteria
to gaze upon this bleached middle age

topography, shimmering up a model beyond
and yet, dislodge the fever of ordained rinse

is the only figure, smuggling, cunning random
watching world of fray, a short trap

hence the boom of habit was the official
willful trawl, an ice-white lament of wrong place

Furry Rocket

furry rocket
all hair
and habitat

rolls undress under
wear
for bang

breath on
a dresser
thief water aura

sock talk
sewing the
room

gown breathing
children in
the flowers

elevator cigar
ette billows in
the cave

spins chest
glass bot
tomed float

freckles the
powdered
crowd

Rooms of Giant Piss

noises wheez
ing & burst
s of pliers o
ver min
neapolis
but no
t like the ot
her wave
s of less
ons brok
en in green
scratch
es of st
ray morn
ings bur
ning out
of art &
the scour
ing word clean
sing left win
gs on comp
ost room
s of gi
ant piss

the rad
io is
on the radio
is a po
et the poe
m is a tong
ue a piranha
it is t
he guts
of citie
s harpo
oning the son
g happy as

jesus
scheming o'er the
blind
ed child
ren the gos
pel trap
s of weather
drank the
mount
ain diet dow
n in the can
yon

Blows the Trope

scope disunity eternal
united but
enter the crest

crest sunk harmonize
blinds inland out
damned commands

waving down
terrifying brief
houseflies taught

bed swale wake
signal sum metaphor
blue sex storm can

so blows allegiance
up my organs
the unmade opposite

inventing the sky
time his field is my
mud of yesterday

dirty them in song
archer smoke spare tassel
remembering arms

return to handle the
spectacle waste but first
everything airplanes bodies

playing garments
the empirical
bind growing either out

mud his means from
the screaming forgotten

summer of window

has that shooting terrain
blinds skin his
image just a dying picture

sunk feet blows the
trope fellow swells
a river wake

of mistakes as in
sea handle heat
burst of wig

cold return ends bodies
wild sun the song
of air organs

dirty for what

Nerve Photo

Gears in the head, a metal
body. Heads are
nevertheless
hoarding us, or dogs
of heads
are.
Shambolic bodies
party
to the south, an
ancient rite of working
our metal fists.

I'm all about American
skies
and photoshopped
flags behind
the furnace, bent
bees' knees
unwinding swag. America
is a concession
rolling over bloody elegies
on plugged lawns
we cheat our
grasses.

We want a new meal
of chocolate
heads, a better brand
of clandestine
hoarding.

Smocked

can room organs— sugar black
into venture
headless from monster
in waterfalls

paint colors cats peel off tenders
melody ships
human libel candies the
stabbed excuse

Warhead

We're bricked as sullen babies
dead as subtle
the till on scraping
still our artificial rhyme;
on to form on
to for
mon tofo rm.

I'm immaculate shivering truth again
like smells ripped through
a slapstick crash, an illegal vision of the
meta-metaphor outlaw.

The repeater ram screams; vanishing
debris of pop through
unknowing down the tussle to
standard typo of evening's importance
where plunders the hole
of takeoff inaccessible
crows.

We're dirt granted cold where
moths the choke-attack,
the posthumous face rolled
in trees.

Flood Machine

Spring is the name he unzips from consciousness
From cupboard out of honest grass-root chaos destruction
The planet dad Christ flashes a rogue shoulder bomb
From my hanging inside I number the words

From cupboard out of honest grass-root chaos destruction
In the righteous dark North implanted with entropy
From my hanging inside I number the words
Backwards like a board of satellites left you witches of
snow

In the righteous dark North implanted with entropy
Bodies dress the random world that yearns its twins
Backwards like a board of satellites left you witches of
snow
Unwrapped eyes in the mountain's planet

Bodies dress the random world that yearns its twins
Guns the flesh paper the rubble of Camp Godlight
Unwrapped eyes in the mountain's planet
Mute wound of clouds opens the can of Spring

The name he unzips from consciousness
Backward pinstripes synch outside the body of Buddha
Unwrapped eyes in the mountain's planet
From my hanging inside I number the words

Nagasaki

o apocalyptic relation whose time
is graffiti

mistaken land
                tattoos spurt

        vernal to the tooling
on which naked is baked

Pluto's Pardoned His Flowers

At the cotton ranch
Ouiji to Devo—
cue everything
by the chateau.

Her parfait blankets
the intolerant South
the poisoned
clouds shred more east.

Let's slumber light in
the flood's echo, the
atrocity of our headache

late dews whose couples
truck birds and name
a valet.

SoHo Morning

bereft of gesture
the glee of light
grows pipes

lashes harmonics

schoolhouse of
skin stops the sub
marine

Suede Moat

who transports words
ashes nape amidst burns it off the
water in
the
drawer phase

you must unsay
the town

basement murmur smell the
whisper on me I luggage out

the paragraph is waning
a sunset finally
of oaks and
a chat
like bracelets
the long harbor's black stairs

what physics of
the rain of taste is plugged

Toddler Prom

drag the hand as the arm
flute spits

chair bound

cookbook of suns
on squeegee wings

swim the stomach
fishlady like

hooves and feathers
no marbled nothing

traffic threads
a sky bulb

traffic of not shoes

Kerosene Trees

Pocket land: eyes breeze
about York, going
the hydraulic

That blew eye unspools

Glass of white silk a sign
of;
My phone trimmed
another long;
Stomp eyes—;

And clink: the post
poetry poems and waves
mistaken lit on
Ibsen's mother are
clothes—doesn't love the
boy son

A Human and Not a Hole

in the stunning footprint
eyes are but chemically
racked
drones in here
through coffins

bone that
floor above air the face defeats
a catastrophe of arrows
in the brutal woods
hoops
the river's pocket
of bombs

a human and not a hole
the cleaving knew
burning buildings
unburied
all the fountains

Snowman

the sickle blue dandelion in mosses against the cardboard
through
pantaloons of morphing american bones

sails of bathhouse promote sleep proctored away quantum
contours
setting moon grayscale time of the city's throat

to be bluster brings burbs touch that outcome tainting the
idea
against swimming upon the pageants

in splash falls crystal of optical withers the colonels like
bears
shapeless in the slip of gravity the only panacea

from the river's brief theories the pitfalls of walking against
a backlogged western silhouette of confirmations

with of mats of chaos the overcoats stuffy with the hostage
of girlfriends
wedlocked on breakfast weather shadows the
hypochondria

gravity of unkempt trickling metropolis to skin the
snowman's mark
black at box bridge her physics sparrows the mischief and
fuselage

poems of confirmation cantaloupe from you who center the
moon circle
into comfort and forgetfulness of physics cradling the page
post

Chainsaw Gender Reveal

rollers of words
in a tree
by the rash
of windows

swallow of bottles
hangs the pickup in

on rain for throated
spooking we've come
to the texture

in the home of
moments in a wood the
falling salt of
singers hinge so

let's murder
the rules

Tom Jones

To marry is guilty love,
nephew. A duel from the waters.
Tommy tutors himself in Westerns
and dead pious conduct torn
into servants.

Marriage to an Irishman, a relative
brags, scares a rascal. Owns
a partridge in the feisty bedroom.
He arrives as a neighbor and
announces his beauty.

Dream Bicycles

the brain fires cry under the blunt
water the black windows wrapped
in the enormous hillside with one
foot in

far somehow the camera
queue rattles out wrapped out in
departure somehow the sea departs
in betrayal sometimes the clues
are missing

that formality of sleep—
icebox strangers dying on brother planes
skin the stunning base of stars

Another Gatsby

1.

polo cocktails red as a Finnish
mansion, she closed

the substitute windows
to the war, fifty absurd

windows, bed into riotous
words, I was a butler of

earthquakes to an enormous
small world

2.

we crushed into a fundamental
afternoon, a sun-strained

room of love, foul glass affair
indeed the heads of women

it was a promising
bungalow

3.

prep-school literary scorn removed
something from herself

wind over the effeminate white rug
of New York, just another fashionable

century of brick and tribute, she
laughed like the prom of snobbish

advice and cardboarded the resemblance
of tradition

4.

I walked through the neighborhood
of sorrows, a yawned porch exempt

from Colonial momentum, post-
house, fluttering curtains

a wingless glowing planet
on this couch

Boner

the preaching shape of the wherewithal
like a boner   like

mode of the school pants accident
the cities' seaweed all over the blood town

he could not god through
scissors or shoes   or
film out like birds to split a monolith

or

utopians' rock trick of the experts
wild in the street streets

Green Rain

Windshield bulge her
onion pinkish curves and
episode. Sky canvas
nests to the wind.

Eye fields watch. Tree
air, her lamb. You are
my over unnatural;
fake pawnshop narrative the
god of dancers the fish is gold.
Paint cottonwoods.

Ambush windblown ground
inside the rubber specimens
my twist demands fleshy
conversations. Beat hand.

A parody topic is retooled
wilderness enforced in
the word sky. And later,
a bath of light swims the
Mojave, excrement spilled
backwards, bloodshot
passengers spike the
knothole.

Tiny Town

whose shoulders hum
in the barren house

acid families concrete
the pages of history

a face of tickets
her hair walked away

from the wearers
of the tiny town

a fuming moment
a stone appeared

on fur half-buried
in the crush

jacket of cotton
black junk buttons wool in

soft sun thin
a roadside boy

took a shining to water
the mean glass sea

and dragged a
railroad in

Keith Higginbotham is the author of Calibration (Argotist eBooks), Theme From Next Date (Ten Pages Press), Prosaic Suburban Commercial (Eratio Editions), and Carrying the Air on a Stick (The Runaway Spoon Press). His collage art has appeared in various publications and in Grace Notes (Unknown Press), a collaborative project with David Tomaloff and Meg Tuite. He lives in South Carolina.

Made in the USA
Columbia, SC
04 May 2023

16042781R00045